JOKE:
A thing that someone says to cause amusement or laughter,
especially a story with a funny punchline.

BAD JOKE:
Keep reading

Students who study Egyptology and plumbing are known as Pharaoh-Faucet Majors.

How does a hippie polygamist count his wives?
1 Mrs. Hippie, 2 Mrs. Hippie…

They arrested that cowboy who wore the paper chaps.
Rustling.

Wonder how many vampires have been run over by people who only use their rearview mirror to back up?

Actors in black & white movies were always putting their lives at risk while driving because they didn't know if the lights were green or red.

I asked my doctor if the spots on my chest were measles or chicken pox. He said he never makes rash decisions.

Word is that, before crowbars were invented, most crows just sat at home and drank.

The advantage of living in Switzerland?
Well, the flag is a big plus.

My wife asked me to stop singing "I'm a Believer" by the Monkees because it was annoying. I thought she was kidding…
Then I saw her face…

A rich businessman brought his Rolls-Royce in for a service. Afterwards, the technician handed him the keys along with a few golf tees.

He said: "Your keys, sir. Oh, and I found these (holding out the tees) in your car. What are they, if you don't mind me asking?"

The businessman thinks, "Oh, he doesn't know golf." And says, "Those are used to rest my balls on when I drive."

The technician thinks, "Man, those folks at Rolls-Royce think of everything!"

If you boil a funny bone, it becomes a laughing stock.
Isn't that humerus?

Combining alphabet soup with ex-lax. Calling it, "Letter Rip."

Do you know why scuba divers roll backwards off of boats?
Because if the rolled forward, they'd just go into the boat.

My Viagra addiction was the hardest time in my life.

The other day, a clown held the door for me.
I thought, "Nice jester."

What do you call a Viking that is full of himself?
A Norse-issist.

I want to be buried with all my record albums from the '70s.
It will be my vinyl resting place.

Me: "I spent my life savings on pasta."
Her: "That's terrible!"
Me: "Nah, it was worth every penne."

Two electric windmills standing in a field. One says to the other, "What kind of music do you like?" The other says, "I'm a huge metal fan."

Bono and The Edge walk into a bar. The bartender says, "Oh no, not you two again."

Remember when we had to smack the TV because it wasn't coming in clearly?
I feel that way about far too many people.

Sometimes I sit on my heels, hug my legs, and just lean forward…
It's how I roll.

What is the number one cause of dry skin?
Towels.

I joined a dating website, but all I seem to be matched up with are arsonists. Guess it's my own fault for using Tinder.

Guy in the grocery store threw a bottle of mayonnaise at me.
I was like, "What the Hellmann?"

A new study says humans eat more bananas than monkeys.
Huh. Can't remember ever eating a monkey.

Why was the cow tired after giving birth? It was decalfeinated.

Whenever I go to a psychic, they're either angry or depressed...
There's just no happy medium.

How do you stop Canadian bacon from curling in your pan?
Ya take away their little brooms, eh?

My doctor said I need to diet and get back to my original weight. I'm
concerned because 7lb., 6oz just doesn't seem realistic.

I just ordered a chicken and an egg on Amazon.
I'll let everyone know.

Don't trust atoms. They make up everything.

I wrapped my Christmas presents early this year but used the wrong
paper. The paper I used said 'Happy Birthday' on it. Didn't want to
waste it, so I just wrote 'Jesus' on it.

My wife and I are learning how to be carpenters. Nothing made so far
but we've only just begun.

People who are afraid of Santa Claus?
Claustrophobic.

What do you call Santa's helpers?
Subordinate clauses.

Why was the elf depressed?
Low elf-esteem.

One Thanksgiving, a man walks into his house with a turkey under his
arm.
He walks up to his wife with it and says, "This is the pig I've been
having sex with."
His wife says, "That's a turkey."
The man replies, "I wasn't talking to you."

What do rednecks do for Thanksgiving?
Pump kin.

What does a stripper eat for Thanksgiving dinner?
Twerky.

What's the difference between Dubai and Abu Dhabi?
The people in Dubai don't like the Flintstones, whereas the people in
Abu Dhabi do.

I just broke up with my girlfriend, Lorraine. She found out that I had been seeing Claire Lee behind her back. It's alright, though… I can see Claire Lee now that Lorraine has gone.

What's Whitney Houston's favorite type of coordination?
Haaaannnd and eeeeyyyyeeee.

I told my wife she was using her eyebrow pencil wrong, making them too high. She looked surprised.

I used to have two Rottweilers, Timex and Rolex.
They were watch dogs.

My wife accused me of being immature. I told her to get out of my fort.

Just read that all the flights from John Lennon Airport in Liverpool were cancelled. Jeez, imagine all the people.

Watched an Australian cooking show. Surprised when the chef made meringue. Australians typically boo meringue.

I went to see a psychic. When I knocked on her door, she yelled "Who is it?" So, I left.

Tried to take my neighbor's kid to the Lego store.
People were lined up for blocks.

What do you call a thunderstorm over Athens?
Greece Lightning

Bruce Willis in a *Lord of the Rings* sequel?
Working title: 'Old Hobbits Die Hard'

Not all construction jobs are enjoyable. For example, enlarging a hole
in a piece of wood is boring, but fastening two pieces of metal
together, that's riveting.

My wife told me to stop impersonating a flamingo.
I had to put my foot down.

Can't believe I got fired from the calendar factory.
All I did was take a day off.

My brother has schizophrenia... but he's good people.

What do you call a wine-colored horse?
Caberneigh

What do you call an unproductive veterinarian?
Dr. Doolittle

I accidentally rubbed ketchup in my eyes. I now have Heinzsight.

My balloon elephant wouldn't fit in the back seat of my car.
So, I had to pop the trunk.

What's blonde and dead in a closet?
The Hide and Seek Champion of 1995.

A man and a woman were having sex in the middle of a dark forest.
After about fifteen minutes, the man finally gets up and says, "Damn,
wish I had a flashlight!"
The woman says, "Me too, you've been eating grass for the past ten
minutes!"

HR: "The only problem is the five-year gap in your resume."
Candidate: "Oh, that's when I went to Yale"
HR: "That is very impressive!"
Candidate: "So, did I get the Yob?"

A guy walks into a bar, tells the bartender that he'll have one mug of
every different beer the place serves. The bartender says, "We have
more than a dozen different beers."
Guy says, "Fine, line 'em up!"
And as the bartender places each of the beers on the bar, the guy
downs each one in big gulps.
Bartender says, "Jeez, you're sure drinking those down fast."
Guy says, "Yeah, well, you'd drink fast, too... if you had what I have."
Bartender asks, "What do you have?"
The guy says, "Forty-seven cents."

"Give it to me! Give it to me!" she yelled. "I'm so wet, give it to me now!"
She can scream all she wants. I'm keeping the umbrella.

I always wanted to be a Gregorian monk, but I never got the chants.

I'm emotionally constipated. I haven't given a shit in days.

If a woman sleeps with ten men, she's a slut, but if a man does it, he's gay. Definitely gay.

There is a new restaurant on the moon.
Good food but no atmosphere.

A chef friend of mine got a gigantic, six-foot-long spoon for Christmas.
As you can imagine, it caused quite a stir.

My wife blocked me from posting too many bird puns.
Well, toucan play that game.

What's the last thing Tickle Me Elmo receives before leaving the factory? Two test tickles.

A guy that was born without eyelids had an operation that used his foreskin as replacements. He's doing okay, just a little cock-eyed.

I'm thinking the guy who invented the umbrella was actually going to call it the brella, but he hesitated.

Why can't you hear a psychologist using the bathroom?
The P is silent!

How do you spot a blind man on a nude beach? It's not hard.

A naked man broke into a church. The police chased him around and finally caught him by the organ.

Just watched a movie called *Broken Ankle*.
It's got a great supporting cast.

Man: "Is that bike for sale?"
Woman: "Yes, it is."
Man: "How low will you go on it?"
Woman: "2mph. Any lower, you'll tip over."

Three pregnant women are at the hospital to find out the gender of their babies.
While chatting in the waiting room, one woman says she's sure hers is a boy because she was on the bottom during sex.
The second one says that hers will be a girl because she was on top.
The third one, a blonde says, "Wow, I can't wait to see my puppies!"

A man comes home carrying a bouquet of flowers. His sarcastic wife says, "I suppose you'll want me to spread my legs now?" The husband says, "Nah, just get a vase."

Nobody went to see that movie *Constipation* because it never came out.

Got fired from the bank. Little old lady asked me to check her balance. So, I pushed her.

What did Yoda say when he saw himself on a 4K TV? HDMI?

How does Moses make his coffee? Hebrews it.

I told the doctor I broke my leg in two places. He said I probably shouldn't go to those places.

When Miley Cyrus is naked and licks a hammer, it's "art" and "music," but when I do it, I'm "wasted" and "have to leave Home Depot."

Karl Marx is a historically important person, granted, but nobody ever mentions his sister, Onya, who invented the starter gun.

Would masturbating while smoking pot be considered masturblazing, weedwhacking, or highjacking?

Did you know that, if you hold a stranger's leg up to your ear, you can actually hear them say, "What the fuck are you doing?"

The local prison implemented a new process where inmates take their own mug shot. They're called Cellfies.

Sad story of the Eskimo who moved into a new igloo. His friends threw him a surprise house-warming party. Now he's homeless.

When I dated a girl who had a twin, people would ask me how I could tell them apart. Simple: Jill would paint her nails purple, and Jack has a dick.

Judging by the size of these chicken fingers, that chicken was somewhere between 18' to 21' tall.

When you choke a Smurf, what color does it turn?

A woman asked me if I like thighs or breasts.
I told her I like a shaved vagina and anal.
Apparently, this isn't an appropriate answer at KFC.

I was going to tell a time-traveling joke, but you didn't like it.

Bigfoot is often confused with Sasquatch. Yeti never complains.

The first rule of passive aggressive club is...
You know what, never mind. It's fine.

The kids have been throwing Scrabble tiles at each other. All fun and
games until someone loses an I.

I opened my pay envelope today and found it was full of parsley.
Someone garnished my wages.

My wife said, "I can think of fourteen reasons to leave you, not to
mention your obsession with tennis."
I replied, "That's 15, love."

I was walking home when a woman rushed up to me and said she
recognized me from a nearby vegetarian restaurant. Which was
strange because I never met herbivore.

The janitor in my building just asked me if I wanted to smoke some
weed with him. I declined. Can't handle high maintenance people.

Grandpa has an addiction to Viagra.
Nobody's taking it harder than Grandma.

The inventor of the snooze button has passed away.
His funeral will take place tomorrow at 8:00, 8:06, 8:12, 8:18 and 8:24.

14

My dryer door keeps popping open during use.
If it does it one more time, that's it... I'm throwing in the towel.

Nobody names their kids Lance these days.
But during the medieval times people were named Lance a lot.

Just found out my new job has a 401K I can participate in, but I'm
really nervous about it. I've never run that far.

The couple next door recently made a sex tape.
They just don't know it yet.

I've got ninety John Lennon CDs and records that I'm going to sell on
eBay. Imagine all the PayPal.

A truck carrying a load of Vicks VapoRub overturned on the highway.
As a result, there is no congestion.

What's the difference between an oral thermometer and a rectal
thermometer? The taste, mostly.

A farmer took his stimulus money and decided to start raising
chickens. Got his money for nothing and his chicks for free.

I once knew a guy who was hooked on brake fluid.
But he said he could stop anytime.

My grief counselor died last week.
She was so good, I didn't even care.

The Norwegian navy is painting barcodes on their ships so when the
ships return to port, they can Scandinavian.

Ordered Chinese food last night and when the Chinese driver pulled
up to deliver it, I went out to meet him.
He started yelling, "Isolate! Isolate!"
I told him, no, I just ordered it fifteen minutes ago.

69% of people find something dirty in every sentence.

I gave up my seat to an elderly person on the bus.
And that's how I lost my job as a bus driver.

A police officer came to the house and asked me where I was
between five and six. I couldn't lie. I told him, "Kindergarten."

Someone tried to convince me to put a cover on my pillow, but I knew
it was a sham.

One of my first memories was getting glasses.
Everything before that was just a blur.

My friend Joe went on the Dolly Parton diet.
It really made Joe lean. Joe lean, Joe lean, Joe lean.

Me: "It's not how many times you fall, it's how many times you get right back up again."
Cop: "Yeah, well, that's not actually how field sobriety tests work."

Vin Diesel eats two meals a day:
1) Breakfast
2) Breakfurious

I've eaten a lot of doughnuts, but I still haven't found the one that makes my brown eyes blue.

When one door closes, another door opens up.
Other than that, it's a pretty good car.

I asked a supermarket worker where they kept the tinned peaches.
"I'll see," he said and walked off. Rude.
Then I asked another worker and got the same reply, "I'll see," and she walked off. Also, rude.
In the end, I gave up and went to find them myself.
I eventually found them in aisle C.

I heard they are making a mind-controlled air freshener.
It makes scents, when you think about it.

The digital camera is a great invention because it allows us to reminisce. Instantly.

At McDonald's, they called out order 867, so I yelled out 5309, but no one laughed. I felt old and ate my burger alone, sitting by myself in the playground section.

How expensive is it to swim with sharks?
It can cost an arm and a leg.

Got a job making plastic Draculas.
There are only two of us on the production line, so I have to make every second count.

There's a new airplane that can't crash. It's made from rubber polymers and just bounces.
Made by Boeing, Boeing, Boeing.

Not happy. I have to work at the museum tonight, moving suits of armor. I hate knight shifts.

I asked the surgeon if I could administer my own anesthetic.
He said, "Sure, knock yourself out."

Do you have a date for Valentine's Day?
Yes, it's February 14th.

I chose Matthew McConaughey as my GPS celebrity voice.
Now I can't turn left.

Being a baby must be traumatizing.
Imagine going to sleep in your bed and then waking up at Target.

As I sit here reflecting on my life and all the people I've lost, I think to
myself: Maybe tour guide was not the job for me.

If anyone gets a message from me about canned meat, do NOT open
it. It's Spam.

I ate a kid's meal at McDonald's today. His mom was furious.

I'm writing a book about all the things I should be doing in my life.
It's an oughttobiography.

I have a step ladder in my garage. Sadly, I never knew my real ladder.

Why was Pavlov's hair so soft?
He conditioned it.

Will glass coffins become popular?
Remains to be seen.

I started saying, "Mucho!" to my Spanish speaking friends.
It means a lot to them.

If I turn into fog, would I be mist?

Boss: "How good are you at PowerPoint?"
Me: "I excel at it."
Boss: "Is that a Microsoft pun?"
Me: "Word."

You can distinguish an alligator from a crocodile by paying attention to whether the animal sees you later or in a while.

Respect people who wear glasses.
They paid money to see you.

My son, Luke, loves that I named my kids after *Star Wars* characters.
My daughter, Chewbacca... not so much.

People say they pick their nose, but I think I'll just stay with the one I was born with.

I asked my friend to spell wonton backwards, but he said not now.

What do you call a priest working out? An exercist.

Ever wonder why, when geese fly, one side of the V is always longer?
That's because there are more geese on that side.

Guy goes into a lumberyard and asks the clerk for a bunch of 2x4s.
Clerk asks, "How long do you want them?"
Guy says, "A while. Building a house."

I can't believe how rude the suppository helpline people are when I ask for directions on how to use.

How much would it cost to buy a singing ensemble?
You mean a choir?
Okay, sorry... how much would it cost to acquire a singing ensemble?

Went swimming at the public pool. Peed in the deep end, but the lifeguard noticed. Blew his whistle so loud I almost fell in.

My favorite exercise is a combination of a lunge and a crunch.
It's called lunch.

Walking home from the bar last night, there was a cheesecake, right on the street. Then, in the middle of the next street, there was a chocolate pudding. The next street after that had an upside-down apple cake. I realized then that the streets were desserted.

How much does it cost for a pirate to get his ears pierced?
A buccaneer.

The swordfish has few predators to watch for as it swims the deep.
Its only worry is the penfish, which is known to be mightier.

Pirate walks into a bar with a paper towel on his head.
Bartender says, "Hey, what gives?"
Pirate says, "Argh, I got a Bounty on me head!"

What's the difference between a burger and a shooting star?
The burger is very meaty, but the other is a little meteor.

My friend David lost his ID. Now he's just Dav.

When you die, what part of your body dies last?
The pupils... They dilate.

My neighbor said my dog was chasing a kid on a bicycle. I was truly
shocked. I didn't know my dog could ride a bike.

I asked my wife if I was the only one she had ever been with. She
said, yes, all the others were nines and tens.

My doctor asked me if I smoke or drink coffee.
I told him I drink it.

I needed a baseball bat to kill this giant mouse I saw.
Unfortunately, I can never go back to Disneyland.

I'm broke, but not the "poor" kind of broke, the classier kind. Broque.

Who's the patron saint of e-mail?
St. Francis of a CC.

What did the father buffalo say when his boy left the herd?
Bison.

I bought a swivel chair for my office. I didn't like it at first but eventually came around.

I made some fish tacos today, but they just ignored them and swam away.

I just saw some red-breasted birds sitting in the sun and selling ice cream. I think they were basking robins.

This girl agreed to go out with me. All I did was buy her a ginger ale. Schwepped her off her feet.

I call my toilet Jim instead of John.
That way, I can tell people I go to the Jim first thing every morning.

What do snakes study when they study the past?
Hisstory.

Ad: Got some old radiators for sale, excellent condition. Will make an ideal housewarming present.

Sixth Sense and *The Titanic* are basically the same movie.
Icy dead people.

When I see someone down, I remind them that it could be worse.
They could be stuck underground and in water.
I just hope they know I mean well.

What does a pessimist ask for when eating cookies?
A half-empty glass of milk.

My grandfather would say, "As one door closes, another one opens."
Great guy, terrible cabinetmaker.

Are advertisements for butter, cream cheese, and peanut butter
considered schmear campaigns?

My friends are upset I steal their kitchen utensils, but it's a whisk I'm
willing to take.

A dwarf inmate was scaling down the prison wall, and as I looked at
him, he sneered at me.
I thought, "Well, that's a little condescending."

Remember when plastic surgery was a taboo subject? Mention it now
and nobody raises an eyebrow.

I had to check myself into the hospital after I mistakenly poisoned
myself. I ate what I thought was an onion, but it was a daffodil bulb.
They say I'll be out sometime in the spring...

A kid who swallowed a handful of coins was in the bed next to mine. I asked how he was, but the nurse said no change yet.

Been trying to break up with my girlfriend, but it's been hard. She's an optician, and every time I tell her I can't see her anymore, she moves an inch closer and says, "How about now?"

I was seriously addicted to the hokey-pokey, but then I turned myself around.

My friend and I were discussing science, and she said she didn't understand cloning.
I said that makes two of us.

I always really wanted to be a plumber, but I realize now it was just a pipe dream.

I'm reading a horror novel in Braille…
Something bad is about to happen. I can feel it!

Air at the gas station used to be free, but now it costs $1.50. Why? Inflation.

I had a dream I was floating in a sea of orange soda. It was kind of a Fanta sea.

My pregnant wife started yelling, out of the blue, "Don't! Won't! Can't!"
No idea what to do with her contractions.

Remember the joke I told you about the chiropractor?
About a weak back.

Met a microbiologist the other day, and it surprised me.
He was a lot taller than I expected.

Why doesn't glue stick to the inside of the bottle?

Who first looked at a cow and said, "I think I'll squeeze these dangly
things and drink whatever comes out!"?
And eggs…?

My dog ate a bunch of Scrabble tiles. He's at the vet now.
No word yet.

A single ant can live for 29 years.
A married ant, much less.

It's a little-known fact that cow farts come from the dairy air.

The man who invented the Ferris wheel never met the man who
invented the merry-go-round.
They traveled in different circles.

My doctor diagnosed me with a rare medical issue, where my veins are on top of each other. I have vericlose veins.

I remember the first time I went camping. It was intense.

What do you call a hundred rabbits walking backwards?
A receding hare line!

It's not a murder of crows without probable caws.

The guy who invented Lifesaver made a mint.

Then there were the Siamese twins who moved to London so the other one could drive for a while.

The suicidal dyslexic that threw himself behind an oncoming train.

New gay sitcom: "Leave it, it's a beaver."

I've been trying to organize a Hide and Seek tournament, but good players are really hard to find.

When life gives you melons, you might be dyslexic.

The problem with kleptomaniacs is that they always take things literally.

My wife just found out I replaced our bed with a trampoline. She hit the ceiling!

Not a big fan of Russian dolls. They're so full of themselves.

A termite walks into the bar and asks, "Is the bar tender here?"

People who constantly use selfie sticks really need to have a good, long look at themselves.

The last thing I want to do is hurt you, but it's still on the list.

I'm reading a book about anti-gravity. It's impossible to put down.

"Doctor, there's a patient on line one that says he's invisible." "Well, tell him I can't see him right now."

The future, the present, and the past walked into a bar. Things got a little tense.

Last night my girlfriend was complaining that I never listen to her... or something like that.

I got a new pair of gloves today, but they're both 'lefts,' which on the one hand is great, but on the other, is just not right.

I didn't think orthopedic shoes would help, but I stand corrected.

It was an emotional wedding. Even the cake was in tiers.

6:30 is the best time on a clock, hands down.

The difference between ignorance and apathy?
I don't know, and I don't care.

If attacked by a mob of clowns, go for the juggler.

Even if a bear has socks and shoes on, he still has bear feet.

A dung beetle walks into a bar and asks, "Is this stool taken?"

Are people born with photographic memories, or does it take time to develop?

A book fell on my head. I only have my shelf to blame.

Four fonts walk into a bar. The bartender yelled, "Hey! We don't like your type in here!"

If you hire an exorcist but don't pay him, do you get repossessed?

A Mexican magician who told his audience that he would disappear on the count of three. He said, "*Uno, dos...*" and poof! He disappeared without a *tres*.

Did you hear about the guy whose whole left side had to be amputated? He's all right now.

A Freudian slip is when you say one thing and mean your mother.

A perfectionist walked into a bar... apparently, the bar wasn't high enough.

My grandfather survived both mustard gas and pepper spray. He was a seasoned veteran.

I went to visit a friend at his new house. He told me to make myself at home. So, I threw him out. I hate visitors.

My husband is mad that I have no sense of direction.
So, I packed up my stuff and right.

"Welcome to Plastic Surgery Anonymous. Nice to see so many new faces here today!"

My favorite movie is *The Hunchback of Notre Dame.* I love a twisted back story.

A bear walks into a bar and says, "Give me a whiskey and... a coke." Bartender asks, "Why the big pause?" The bear shrugs. "I'm not sure; I was born with them."

I bought some shoes from a drug dealer. I don't know what he laced them with, but I've been tripping all day.

The man who created autocorrect has died. Restaurant in peace.

When I first got a universal remote control, I thought, "This changes everything."

It was hard to believe that the road worker was stealing from the job, but when they went to his home, all the signs were there.

There are three kinds of people: Those who can count, and those who can't.

My first job was working in an orange juice factory, but I got canned. I just couldn't concentrate.

I'll never forget the words my grandfather said before he kicked the bucket. He said, "Grandson, watch how far I can kick this bucket."

I was in Paris and went to a bar where this French guy made me drink and smoke. Pierre pressure.

There's a ton of crap on the TV these days. Maybe I shouldn't leave the birdcage on top of it.

My boss says I exaggerate the time I work now that we're remote. Well, I'd like to see him work 12 days a week, 422 days of the year.

I have a friend who's trying to set the world record for masturbating. He may just pull it off.

Eskimos eat whale meat and blubber. Well, you'd blubber, too, if all you could eat was whale meat.

I got a job as a deep-sea diving instructor but had to quit. I'm just not good under pressure.

I was at the gym and decided to jump on the treadmill. People were staring, so I started running instead.

Can someone tell me what 'concise' means? However, I need the answer to be short, brief, and to the point.

I saw a kidnapping near my house the other day… but I just shook him a little, and he woke up.

Going through airport security, and the guy asked, "Do you have any firearms?"
Evidently, "Why, what do you need?" is not the right answer.

They're selling an image of Jesus that pops up on your computer when you haven't used it for a while. It's called a screen savior.

Not sure I believe in the Big Bang Theory but I definitely believe in the Big Foreplay Theory.

Got a job as a shepherd, but I don't think I'll last that long. Every time I go to count the flock, I fall asleep.

How many mimes have died because no one believed they were choking?

My wife laughed when I slipped on a banana peel.
Hey, we ran out of condoms!

Article in *Esquire* called "100 things to do before you die." Weirdly enough, "yell for help" wasn't one of them.

My friend told me the highlight of his life was climbing Mount Everest and that it was all downhill from there.

Everyone at work loved my volcano joke.
The whole place erupted.

Chinese couple in bed. She says "I want 69!"
He says, "Beef and Broccoli?"

I was arrested at work today. Evidently, taking your work home is
frowned upon at the bank.

Thought it was inappropriate that, when the candle factory burned
down, everyone just stood there, singing 'Happy Birthday.'

Played poker last night with an origami expert. Boring. He kept folding.

I've been Employee of the Month five months running.
Being self-employed is great!

I used to date a girl with one leg who worked at a brewery.
She was in charge of the hops.

My wife left me after I spent all our savings on a penis extension.
Said she couldn't take any more.

I had a hamster that died from lack of exercise.
Just didn't have the wheel to live.

I have a rare brain malfunction that makes me need to make
everything sound mysterious… or do I?

Dropped some LSD, and now my pupils look massive.
Probably shouldn't trip while I'm teaching.

I hear reincarnation is making a comeback.

When I worked as a waiter, I used to hate when people asked, "How
do you prepare the chicken?"
I'd reply that we were straight with them: "You're going to die."

Ordered Peking duck at a Chinese restaurant, a whole duck. It was
great until they brought the bill.

My dad's motto was "Work hard, play hard!" He was addicted to
Viagra.

Make-up sex with my girlfriend is usually great. Although, I think I may
be allergic to the eyeliner she uses.

We hired a Brazilian housekeeper. Upstairs is a mess, but downstairs
is neat and trim.

A weasel walks into a bar. The bartender laughs and says, "I've never
served a weasel. What can I get you?"
"Pop!" goes the weasel.

The inventor of autocorrect has died. His funnel is tomato.

A cheese factory exploded in France. Da brie was everywhere.

What's a contortionist from the Philippines?
A Manila Folder.

Where does okra come from?
Okrahoma

Then there was the dog that went to the flea market and stole the show.

A friend became a mime. Haven't heard from him since.

I'm in a procrastinator's support group, but the meeting keeps getting postponed.

Of all the different blood groups, Type Os make the most spelling mistakes.

I really need to beat this helium addiction before I get carried away.

The worst thing about having ADD and OCD is forgetting to wash your hands fifty times a day.

I've been carb-loading for the last thirty years in case I ever need to go on a 5,000-mile run.

I've begun day trading. I have an extra Thursday if anyone has a Sunday they don't want.

I can't watch Larry, Moe, and Curly anymore. I've developed Stooge fright.

High-wire artists hate it when their cable goes out.

I never have success on Amazon. Today, my cart had a defective wheel.

Went on a scavenger hunt. Did okay. Shot three scavengers.

As you get older, you take life with a grain of salt… and a slice of lemon and a shot of tequila.

Our mother was very overprotective. We could only play, "Rock, Paper."

If you put instant coffee in a microwave, you can go back in time.

On our ninth date, we watched *Batman* on DVD. So it went: Dinner, Dinner, Dinner, Dinner, Dinner, Dinner, Dinner, Dinner, BATMAN!

All-knight diners were big in the Renaissance period.

Police have confirmed that the man who tragically fell from the roof of an 18-floor nightclub was not a bouncer.

Sad about Sea World not being able to mate those two dolphins they received. Guess they just didn't click.

She told me her hair needed a good teasing, so I laughed and told her it was ugly and smelled bad.

I took a pole and found out 100% of the people in the tent were pissed when it collapsed.

I must be allergic to peanuts. I break out in a rash every time I get my paycheck.

The handshake was developed in the Middle Ages to show one meant no harm and had no weapon. It was a feudal gesture.

Guy had an old-fashioned radio for sale, just a dollar. $1! Only thing was, the volume was stuck on full tilt. I don't think I can turn that down.

Love that Peter Pan joke. Never gets old.

Oh, I'm sorry. Did the middle of my sentence interrupt the beginning of yours?

So, if a cow stops producing milk is it a milk dud or an udder failure?

We have a beautiful little girl named after my mom. Little Passive Aggressive Psycho turns five tomorrow.

A woman shouldn't have children after forty. Because, really, forty kids are more than enough.

Someone stole the toilets out of the police station. The cops have nothing to go on.

My friend had to be committed. He was a Morse code expert, and I took him to see *Riverdance*.

They stopped making the Yugo because the Czech engine light was always on.

I used to have a fear of hurdles. I got over it.

Little known fact: Lassie liked honeydews and was always depressed. She was a melon collie.

Whenever I read about someone being attacked by a shark, I think, "Didn't they hear the music?"

I read about a party of archeologists that was searching for a lower leg bone. Quite the shindig.

Sirius, the Dog Star, is moving towards earth at a rate of 9 miles per second. Someday, we could be in Sirius trouble.

I love looking at the moon. Half-moon, full moon, crescent moon. Guess it's just a phase I'm going through.

Can circumcisions be done at any age, or is there a cut-off date?

In Vegas, churches often receive casino chips in the tithe basket. Because they can't enter the casinos themselves to cash them in, they ask a Franciscan order of friars to make the exchange. They are referred to as chip monks.

The Wisconsin couple got married at the cheese factory where they both worked. Tragically, the photographer was badly injured when a ton of cheese fell on him.
Well, the wedding party did try to warn him.

How many mice does it take to screw in a light bulb?
Two, but it's anybody's guess how they got inside the lightbulb.

I have an inferiority complex. And not a particularly good one.

Astronaut 1: "I can't find any milk for the coffee."
Astronaut 2: "In space, no one can. Here, use cream."

I was born a pessimist. My blood type is B-negative.

When a fellow mime passes away, do the other mimes have a brief
moment of talking?

My grandfather was responsible for downing thirty planes in WWII.
Worst airplane mechanic the Luftwaffe ever had.

Feeling better since I switched from coffee to OJ in the morning.
My wife thinks it's the vitamin C, but I'm thinking it's the vodka.

Not a big fan of giraffes... always get the feeling they're looking down
on me.

This smokin' hot girl asked me for my number today!
And all I had to do was hit her car with my car.

My buddy and I were in a bar, drinking. I pointed across the room at
two really haggard old guys and told him, "That's us in ten years."
He said, "That's a mirror."

Do the other birds ask penguins to get them drinks at parties?

I need a dog that can find anything. I need a Labragoogle.

"Doctor, I can't stop singing 'What's New, Pussy Cat'!"
"I think it's a case of Tom Jones Syndrome."
"Is that common?"
"It's not unusual."

Heat makes things expand. So, I'm not overweight, just overheated.

I was badly hurt last week in a game of hide-and-seek.
They admitted me to the ICU.

I've started investing in stocks... beef, chicken, vegetable.
I hope to become a boullionaire.

I used to work in a blanket factory. It folded.

"Let me make this perfectly clear."
Me, before I start cleaning a window.

Tried that new Mexican restaurant for the lactose intolerant:
No Whey, Jose's.

There's a national coin shortage. Evidently, during the pandemic,
everyone started a swear jar.

My mechanic told me he keeps have nightmares about mufflers and can barely sleep. He's exhausted.

A good friend told me I make people uncomfortable by violating personal space. It was a hurtful thing to say. Completely ruined our bath.

I stayed up all night wondering where the sun had gone. And then it dawned on me.

I thought my new girlfriend was the one until I looked in her dresser. There was a nurse's outfit, a French maid's outfit, and a cop's uniform. So, I knew: If she can't hold down a job, it's over.

I'm having a ridiculous amount of anxiety that I'm taking too much Viagra. Worried stiff.

Got kicked out of the park for arranging squirrels by height. People hate it when you critter-size.

I put up a high voltage electric fence around the property. The neighbors are dead against it.

The Grammy Awards are in April, but I don't see myself watching old ladies playing Mah-Jongg for two hours, do you?

This hot girl I know bought a taser. She's stunning!

I like booking passage on a cruise ship, positioning myself near the buffet tables, and seeing the heaps of food people take. I call it 'whale watching.'

When I worked at the mall, I saw the Apple store get robbed. Ended up being an iWitness.

I bring my wife her morning tea in my pajamas. But is she grateful? No, says she'd rather have it in a cup.

I asked the gym instructor, "Can you teach me to do splits?" He said, "How flexible are you?" I said, "Well, Tuesdays are bad, but every other day works."

Two monkeys were getting into the bath. One said, 'Oo, oo, oo, aah, aah, aah.' The other replied, "So, put some cold in then."

As a scarecrow, people say I'm outstanding in my field. But hay, it's in my jeans.

Next year I am going to hire the same landscaper I had this year. He was so easy to get a lawn with.

One cannibal to another: "What's eating on you?" "Oh, nothing, I'm just fed up with people."

Football players aren't allowed to go to bakeries on game day. Coaches worry about too many turnovers.

Went to my first Stalkers Help group. Surprised I knew a lot of people there. They didn't know me.

Why do people use metaphors that are physically impossible? It makes my blood boil.

More people would be open to the vaccine if it had been described as installing virus protection software.

Flight attendants still show passengers how to buckle a seatbelt. Is that in case someone on the flight might not have been in a car since the '50s?

Not saying we don't love each other anymore, but the only time my wife runs her fingers through my hair is when she cleans the shower drain.

I didn't use the colander correctly. My wife gave me a restraining order.

Someone has been stealing the wheels off of squad cars, and the police are working tirelessly to find the culprit.

We nicknamed a guy at work 'Foreskin.'
He disappears when things get hard.

I was driving and had an accident with a magician.
Guy came out of nowhere.

I went hiking this morning. Saw a rabbit in front of a candle, making shadows of people on a tree.

The first rule of Thesaurus Club is you don't talk about, mention, speak of, discuss, orate, recite, or chat about Thesaurus Club.

I tried to be a professional fisherman but discovered I couldn't live on my net income.

Finally decided I needed Gamblers Anonymous and called to find out the time of the next meeting.
Ten to one.

Someone broke into the local bagel shop. Must have picked the lox.

Got thousands of letters deliver to my mailbox.
Last time I order a dictionary from IKEA.

I first realized I was dyslexic when I went to a toga party dressed as a goat.

After years of costly research, a group of military scientists have discovered why the dinosaurs went extinct. It's because they all died.

Carpe Diem—"Seize the Day" in Latin. Also in Latin: *Projice Eam*—"Throw it Back."

My body is a temple. Looks and feels like something destroyed by the Romans 2,500 years ago.

I tried to share a sandwich with a homeless guy I saw sitting in a bench. He got pissed and told me to get my own.

I was supposed to be in the wedding party but got kicked out. Is it wrong to refer to the rehearsal dinner as 'The Last Supper'?

When the clock factory burned down, there was a fair amount of second-hand smoke.

Guy asked me if I was interested in investing in the Egyptian Tourism industry. Almost did it until I realized it was just another pyramid scheme.

During the lockdown, I got addicted to square dancing on Zoom. Now I'm looking for a good two-step program to help me get over it.

Just bought the latest version of Monopoly. Only change is they added 'Government Bailout' cards to 'Chance' and 'Community Chest.'

Vacationing in Bermuda, I went to hear a symphony.
Weirdly, the guy playing the triangle disappeared.

Fascinated by the news story of that guy they caught counterfeiting and how he paid his bail with ten crisp, new $5,000 bills.

I would never fly Virgin. I want a plane that'll go all the way.

My mother had to have a Caesarean when I was born. Didn't affect me other than, when I leave the house, I go through a window instead of the front door.

Deja Moo: the feeling you've heard this bullshit before.

It starts with a little white lie. Then they get bigger and easier to tell. Then, finally, you pass the Bar exam.

Have you ever looked at what's in all those bottles of hand sanitizer? The first thing on the ingredient list is 'paranoia.'

My apathy is at an all-time whatever...

Tried runway modeling once. It was a disaster, and now I've been banned from the airport.

If I had to describe myself in one word, I would say, "Bad at following directions."

Got arrested and the lawyer wanted a retainer. I'll be damned if I'm gonna pay for his dental work.

My dad was behind bars for twenty-five years. Then again, he was a bartender.

Superman. Big deal. Anyone can stop a speeding bullet... once.

Went to the pharmacy and told the pharmacist, "I have an awful headache. Can you make something up for me?" He said, "Sure. Elvis was in here last week."

I was in the mall and saw a kid on a leash. The mother got offended when I asked if it was a rescue.

Teaching hobbits to play baseball. Bilbo would make a great catcher. He can't really Frodo.

I've got a Master's degree in philosophy but got fired from my job for asking, "Why do you want fries with that?"

You can smoke weed in the rain but don't in hail.

Experts are saying smoking pot affects your short-term memory.
And who knows what it does to your short-term memory.

My bathroom reading is a bio of the Velvet Underground.
It's a Lou Reed.

Polygamy. The ancient art of folding parrots.

Sponges grow in the ocean. Can you imagine how deep it would be if
that didn't happen?

Got a new job working for a tree-trimming company.
I'm a branch manager.

A slice of Apple pie…
In Jamaica: $2.50
In Haiti: $2.00
In Barbados: $3.00
In the Bahamas: $4.50!
These are the pie rates of the Caribbean.

I have a French friend who's a sound technician.
And a Czech one, too.
And a Czech one, too.

A flock of seabirds in California flew over a marijuana testing site when they were burning the plants.
Not one tern was left unstoned.

What did they yell at Edgar Alan Poe when he nearly walked into a tree?
Poetry!

People think learning Roman numerals is hard, but by the time you get to 159, everything CLIX.

Once upon a time, there was a king who was only twelve inches tall.
He was a terrible king but a great ruler.

Can you think of anything worse than being scalped?
Not off the top of my head.

I bought a newt as a pet. His name is Tiny because he's my newt.

Just lost a close friend who worked for forty years at a sheep-shearing plant. Died in the wool.

Got a job at the guillotine factory. Be heading there tomorrow.

My girlfriend and I often laugh about how competitive we are.
But I laugh more.

"I have a split personality," said Tom, being frank.

I watched a documentary on marijuana yesterday.
That's probably how I'll watch all documentaries from now on.

After a lengthy court battle, Clark Kent lost custody of his kids.
He only gets to see them with super-vision.

Guy goes into a pet store and asks for a dozen bees.
Clerk counts out thirteen and hands him the bag.
Guy says, "That's too many!"
Clerk says, "Sale today. That's a freebie."

There's a new bird flu variant called Cherpies. It's a canariel disease,
and it untweetable.

"Yeah, I pretty much never sit by the pool anymore."—Marco Polo

Waiting to get adjusted at the chiropractor, I paged through some
magazines, but all they had were back issues.

My girlfriend is obsessed with taking blurry pictures of herself while
taking a shower. Serious selfie steam issues.

My father was a man of few words. I remember one time he said to me, "Son."
Then I asked him, "Dad, are we pyromaniacs?"
He said, "Yes, we arson."

What do you call a pig with laryngitis? Disgruntled.

Why do bees stay in their hives during winter? 'Swarm.

Hugh burned down the church from which the monks sold the flowers they grew because only Hugh can prevent florist friars.

I once worked at a cheap pizza shop to get by. I kneaded the dough.

My friends and I have named our band Duvet. It's a cover band.

I lost my girlfriend's audiobook, and now I'll never hear the end of it.

I got over my addiction to chocolate, marshmallows, and nuts.
I won't lie, it was a rocky road.

What do you say to comfort a friend who's struggling with grammar?
There, their, they're.

I went to the toy store and asked the assistant where the Schwarzenegger dolls are, and he replied, "Aisle B, back."

What did the surgeon say to the patient who insisted on closing up their own incision?
"Suture self."

I've started telling everyone about the benefits of eating dried grapes. It's all about raisin awareness.

My neighbor, a dentist, had us over for dinner. The fish was excellent, but I passed on the tartar sauce.

Mistakenly sprayed deodorant in my mouth. Now I speak with a weird Axe scent.

She was only a whisky-maker, but he loved her still.

A rubber-band pistol was confiscated from an algebra class because it was a weapon of math disruption.

No matter how much you push the envelope, it'll still be stationery.

A dog gave birth to puppies near the road and was cited for littering.

A grenade thrown into a kitchen in France would result in Linoleum Blownapart.

Two silk worms had a race. They ended up in a tie.

A hole has been found in the nudist camp wall. The police are looking into it.

A sign on the lawn at a drug rehab center said: "Keep off the Grass."

When cannibals ate a missionary, they got a taste of religion.

If you jumped off the bridge in Paris, you'd be in Seine.

A vulture, carrying two dead raccoons, boards an airplane. The stewardess looks at him and says, "I'm sorry, sir, only one carrion allowed per passenger."

Two fish swim into a concrete wall. One turns to the other and says, "Dam!"

Two Eskimos sitting in a kayak were chilly, so they lit a fire in the craft. Unsurprisingly, it sank, proving, once again, that you can't have your kayak and heat it, too.

Two hydrogen atoms meet. One says, "I've lost my electron."
The other says, "Are you sure?"
The first replies, "Yes, I'm positive."

Did you hear about the Buddhist who refused Novocain during a root-canal? His goal: transcend dental medication.

Yeesh. It's been six months since I ordered "How to Scam People Online," and it's still not here.

I went to see an acupuncturist today. When I got home, my voodoo doll was dead.

I went to my doctor with a list of twelve ailments. He only looked into the 2nd, 3rd, 5th, 7th, and 11th ailments. He's my primary physician.

Couples Councilor: "What brings you here today?"
Wife: "I can't take it anymore. He's just so literal!"
Husband: "My truck."

My sister wanted to marry a mailman, but our parents wouldn't letter.

Male lions will often eat other lions if they're starving. Just have to swallow their pride.

Times are so tough. Had to take a job as a waiter to put food on the table.

Lived on a houseboat for a while and dated a girl living on the next houseboat over. Didn't really work out... we drifted apart.

Return of the Jedi is not possible without the receipt of the Jedi.

Even though I went bald years ago, I still carry a comb.
I just can't part with it.

Just before I die, I'm going to swallow three bags of popcorn kernels.
Gonna be a fun cremation.

Bought a fish tank because of the calming effect on the brain.
You know, indoor fins.

My kids glued together our only deck of cards. I can't deal with it.

You're on a horse, going full speed. There's a giraffe right next to you and a lion chasing you. What do you do?
Get your drunk ass off the carousel.

Every morning, I tell the people I work with I'm going jogging on the lunch break. Then I don't.
Kind of a running joke.

If you get abducted by a group of mimes, they will do unspeakable things to you.

The serial flasher who thought about retiring but decided to stick it out another year.

New superhero: Aluminum Man. Doesn't really stop the bad guys, just foils their plans.

I saw a chicken wearing tennis shoes.
They were ReBock, Bock, Bocks.

A 9-year-old girl disappeared after using a moisturizer that makes you look ten years younger.

Britain calls it a 'lift,' but Americans call it an 'elevator.'
Guess we're just raised differently.

The world's strangest competition to see who could lose the most muscle mass over a six-week period.
The winner got atrophy.

Perfect pitch in music?
When you throw an accordion in a dumpster and it hits a banjo.

My doctor diagnosed me with anxiety and constipation.
I'm worried shitless.

My dyslexic grandfather was a baker in the army.
Known for going in, buns glazing.

My wife and I went out for Mexican food, then to a museum.
It was a real artsy-fartsy evening.

People know Jason Bourne but few know he has a brother in
Australia, Mel.

Just broke up with my girlfriend. She was a baker… too kneady.

My wife says I don't pay her enough attention…
Well, something like that.

Saw an ad for burial plots and thought, "That's the last thing I need."

Reading about the Middle Ages and discovered that guillotine
salesman was one of the hardest jobs… totally cut throat.

Bought the wife a new fridge for her birthday. I know, appliances for a
birthday? Well, you should have seen her face light up when she
opened it.

Xerox & Wurlitzer have merged and will be making reproductive
organs.

The older I get, the harder it is to diet. The only way I could lose
twenty pounds is at a British casino.

Bought my wife this slinky dress. Man, she looked so cool going down the stairs.

Our toddler puts everything in his mouth. Yesterday, he was chewing on a bunch of electrical wires... had to ground him.

Had a vasectomy because I didn't want any kids, but when I got home, they were still there.

How fun would it be if the people whose job it is to rescue returning astronauts wore ape costumes?

Slight change to the birds and the bees:
Small babies are delivered by a stork. Heavier ones require a crane.

Learned on one of those family tree sites that my great-great-grandfather tried prospecting... didn't pan out.

Maybe when you see a deaf couple holding hands, it's not actually romantic. Maybe they just want each other to shut up.

Discovered this is a not a good pickup line:
"You have the same soft skin as my sister."

Deer balls is the cheapest meat you can find... under a buck.

Why was the cross-eyed teacher fired?
She couldn't control her pupils.

Went to a restaurant and ordered their special, Napoleon Chicken.
When it came, there was no meat, just a carcass.
I asked the waitress, "What's this?!"
She said, "The boney part."

Juan and Juanita were married a long time. Then one day, Juanita
caught Juan cheating on her. Blinded by jealousy and rage, she took
out a gun and shot him. Cause of death? A hole in Juan.

Went out to eat the other night. The waitress asked, "Box for your
leftovers?"
I said, "Hey, if you want 'em that bad, you just keep 'em."

Went to a disco this weekend. They played 'The Twist,' so I did. They
played 'Jump,' so I did.
Got kicked out when they played 'Come On, Eileen'.

When happens when chemists die? Apparently, they barium.

Quit my job at the helium factory.
I will not be spoken to in that tone of voice.

I told my wife I'm losing my hearing. She asked me what the
symptoms are. I said, "A cartoon family with Homer, Marge, Lisa, and
Bart."

I have an irrational fear of umbrellas, but I'm seeing a therapist. She's getting me to open up.

Bought a horse. Wife said, "What you going to do it with it?"
I said, "Race it."
She said, "My money's on the horse."

Elon Musk and Bill Gates in a joint venture to create a medication that treats erectile dysfunction. They have decided to call it 'Elongates'.

Got into a taxi, and the driver asked, "Do you mind if I put some music on?"
I said, "No, not at all."
He said, "Kiss?"
I said, "Let's start with the music and see how we feel."

If two gorillas share an Amazon account, are they considered prime apes?

My car only runs every other day. Might be the alternator.

Read about a guy that fell into an upholstery machine! The good news is he's fully recovered.

I was dating a girl that sold magazines, but I had to break up with her. Too many issues.

Charles Dickens walked into a bar. The bartender asked, "What'll you have?"
Dickens replied, "I'd like a martini."
The bartender said, "Olive or twist?"

I asked the Librarian, "Do you have *Great Expectations*?"
She said, "I did but ended up working here instead."

I found a recipe for Moroccan dinner rolls. Called for thyme, but what I had was past the sell date. Used it anyway.
Really loved that old thyme Moroccan rolls.

Do songbirds get pissed at hummingbirds for not bothering to learn the lyrics?

Trying to give up using sexual innuendo but it's hard.
So, so hard.

My grandfather used to have a dairy farm. Every morning, he dressed up all the cows before bringing them in to be milked.
Man, they were just so cute in their Milk Duds.

When bored, I sometimes call a Best Western hotel. When they answer, "Best Western?", I say, "True Grit" and hang up.

I'VE DECIDED TO WRITE ALL THESE JOKES IN CAPITALS FROM NOW ON. I WROTE THIS ONE IN ALBANY.

Everyone in the condo complex wears sweaters that are a size too small for them. Well, they said it was a tight-knit community.

Apple has delayed releasing their computerized car. Evidently, they're having trouble installing Windows.

I went to the library to get a medical book on abdominal pain. Somebody had ripped the appendix out.

How do the heart, liver, and lungs all fit in your body? Organization.

For years I was against organ transplants.
Then I had a change of heart.

You can hear the blood in your veins if you listen varicosely.

My cardiologist keeps sending me X-rays of his chest. A bit weird, but it shows his heart is in the right place.

I think I am becoming a social vegan… I'm avoiding meets.

What's a bedpan in Russia? A Poo-tin

I think my grandmother is 80% Irish. He name is Iris.

Visiting Minnesota recently, I accidentally dropped a full jar of Hellmann's on my foot. Fortunately, the Mayo Clinic is there.

My brother has been trying to make my dad wear his hearing aid, but he just won't listen.

A prince grew weary of his life. He told his advisors he wanted to give up the crown but asked to continue making laws.
One of the advisors said in response, "Sorry, my prince, you can't abdicate and edict, too."

I was sitting on the edge of the bed last night, pulling off my boxers. My wife said, "Jeez, you really spoil those dogs!"

My doctor told me I'd been using the suppositories he prescribed all wrong. It was a tough pill to swallow.

Sometimes, I get this urge to break out singing 'The Lion Sleeps Tonight'. I fight it off, but I know it's just a whim away, a whim away, a whim away…

The scientist who cloned his first human being, then pushed him out a window for making inappropriate remarks has been charged with making an obscene clone fall.

Siri kept calling me Shirley today.
I was annoyed until I realized I had left my phone in airplane mode.

Chinese Takeout: $12
Tip: $2
Discovering they left out a major part of the order?
Riceless

My email password has been hacked again.
That's the third time I've had to rename the dog.

I do really well in marathons but just poorly in the 100-yard dash.
Guess I'm better off in the long run.

My doctor said that at my age, I should install a bar in the shower. Just
have to figure out how to keep the shot glasses from getting wet.

I was in a bar, sitting next to two very large women who were clearly
foreigners.
I said, "Cool accents. Are you ladies from Scotland?"
One looked at me and said, "Wales, you idiot!"
I said, "Okay, sorry. Are you two whales from Scotland?"
That's when the trouble started.

Just in: A ship carrying a cargo of yo-yos has sunk. 27 times.

We ran out of ketchup, so I told my kids to put it on the grocery list.
Now I can't read the other items.

A pessimist sees a dark tunnel. An optimist sees light at the end of the tunnel. A realist sees a freight train.
The train driver sees three idiots, standing in the middle of the tracks.

Got a letter from the company that financed my ladder:
"Promptly make a payment or steps will be taken!"

My local bakery still has their "Help Wanted" sign up. I went in and asked why. Turnovers.

Someone suggested using WD-40 to get rid of our mice problem.
Said it doesn't kill them, just stops the squeaking.

The reason I went to the Himalayan Horse races?
Tibet.

I used to have an unnatural fear of speed bumps, but I'm getting over it.

My pet mouse Elvis was found dead in the kitchen.
He was caught in a trap and couldn't get out.
It was suspicious.

In the old west, they mounted lanterns onto their horses so they could ride when it got dark. The first saddle light navigation.

Genie: "I shall grant you three wishes."
Man: "I wish for a world without lawyers."
Genie: "Done, you have no more wishes."
Man: "But you said three!"
Genie: "So, sue me!"

I was in my garden when my neighbor looked over the fence and asked, "What are you doing?"
I told her, "I'm putting all my plants in alphabetical order."
She said, "Really? How do you find the time?"
"That's easy, its right next to the sage."

Had a new building constructed for my business. Rooms only have a 5-foot ceiling. Want to keep a low overhead.

Bought my friend an elephant for his room. He said, "Thanks."
I said, "Don't mention it."

I arrived at the restaurant early for a meal with friends.
The hostess asked, "Would you mind waiting for a while?"
"Not at all," I replied.
She said, "Good. Take these two steaks over to the couple by the window. Then start clearing tables four and seven."

"I've got a half-sister."
"Oh, different fathers?
"Shark attack."

The blind man who fell down a hole? He couldn't see that well. It was a day well spent, but a hole lot of trouble.

Started a new book about a group of insects who take over a European city. Rome ants novel.

On a cold winter morning, a wife texts her husband at work: "Windows frozen, won't open."
He texts back, "Gently pour hot water over it and see if that helps."
She texts back, "Computer is completely fucked now."

No such thing as a cheap circumcision. It's just a rip off.

Lost my pizza cutter so I used a Bryan Adams CD. Cuts like a knife.

Sad. RIP, Pillsbury Doughboy.
From a yeast infection and constant, traumatic pokes in the belly. He was 71. Survived by wife, Play, and three children, John, Jane and Dill. Funeral will be at 3:50 for twenty minutes.

I love putting on warm underwear, fresh from the dryer... then looking around the laundromat and guessing who they belong to.

Deja Moo: The feeling that you've heard this bullshit before.

I just got a new security job. I was told to watch the office at night. I'm on season eight, but I don't get what this has to do with security.

The last time I had faith in the news was when they played with Huey Lewis.

I'm constantly fighting the urge to strip naked and run around. I find Windex works best to stop streaking.

The cashew business I started is doing so well. I was able to hire someone to make deliveries. He drives me nuts.

My WhatsApp app is not working, so I googled companies that could help fix it. Settled on a group called 'Bugs Bunny,' that advertises itself as a WhatsApp doc.

The contortionist competition in Las Vegas got canceled. Huh. That'll leave quite a few people bent out of shape.

What a moron. Guy shows up at church dressed like as a cheerleader. Evidently, someone who stutters told him it was Pom-Pom Sunday.

Hear about the cow who works for Uber? Cattle drives.

When my wife is sad, I let her color in my tattoos… a shoulder to crayon.

Texan: "Where do you come from?"
Ivy League Grad: "I, sir, hail from a place where we do not end our sentences with a preposition!"
Texan: "Oh, okay. So, where do you come from, Asshole?"

My friend got kicked out of the church for claiming Jesus spoke with a lisp. Major slap in the faith.

Went to buy a couch and the salesman said the one I looked at would seat five people without a problem.
I passed. I don't know five people without a problem.

Got a private tour of the Vatican. They showed me a natural fountain inside they say never stops flowing.
Apparently, the Pope's spring's eternal.

My wife says I'm guilty of interjecting coffee puns into every conversation...
I asked, "On what grounds?"

Getting old. Was a time a new hip joint meant a place to go on weekends.

Bought a new stick deodorant. The instructions said: "Remove cap and push up bottom." It hurts to walk, but when I fart, the room smells lovely.

I got into bed and started touching her.
She said, "You're drunk!"
I asked, "How do you know?"
She said, "Because you live next door!"

Walking down the street with my two pet tigers when a cop stopped
me and told me to take them to the zoo. Saw me again a week later
and was upset because I still had my tigers.
He said, "I thought I told you to take those cats to the zoo?"
I told him I did. That we had so much fun there that today, I was taking
them to a museum.

Daffy Duck finished shopping. At the checkout he asked for a carrier
bag.
The checkout girl asked, "Shall I put it on your bill?"
Daffy replied, "Don't be thupid. I could thuffocate."

My urologist said my prostrate was in good shape.
I was deeply touched.

I come from a family of failed magicians. I have two half-sisters.

I sometimes wonder what our parents did to keep from being bored
before the internet, social media, smart phones, and 800 channels. I
think I'll ask my nine sisters and eight brothers.

I joined an amateur autopsy club.
Every Wednesday is Open Mike Night!

Had lunch with a friend, and I ordered a tongue sandwich. She said
she would never eat that; it comes from a cow's mouth.
I told her to enjoy her eggs.

I've been suffering from seizures for six months.
So far, they've taken my car, my boat, and my house.

When two egotists meet, it's an I for an I.

It's how you look at it. Some say bacon is not healthy.
I say it's a meat-flavored fruit rollup.

Three moles are in a tunnel.
The first mole says, "I smell sugar!"
The second mole says, "I smell cinnamon!"
The third mole says, "I smell molasses!"

Just read that the guy from the circus who gets shot from a cannon is
retiring. Gonna be hard to find a replacement of his caliber.

A friend staying at the house asked me if I had any Q-tips.
I said, "Yeah, first I make a circle, and then I make a little line out of
the bottom."

Sea captains really don't like crew cuts.

The look on the cashier's face was priceless when she scanned the packet of bird seed and I asked her how long it takes to grow a bird after planting.

Boss: "Okay, we're gonna start random drug testing."
Me: "Okay, but I draw the line at crack and heroin."

Opened a new store, selling shoes that are only size 16 and up. In this economy? Let me tell you, it was no small feat.

Special presentation of *Wizard of Oz* on the ID channel: "Young girl is mysteriously transported to a strange land. She kills the first person she meets, and then teams up with three strangers to kill again."

Went to a fundraiser dinner last night for hemorrhoid research. It wasn't formal but, everyone had to wear a Tucks.

The dating website for chickens was short-lived. They shut it down for good. Guess they had trouble making hens meet.

Had a bad experience when I drove through Prague. I went by a truck carrying a trampoline with a guy on it, doing tricks. Got a ticket for passing a bouncing Czech.

I've finished reading a book about the world's greatest basement. Gonna be a best cellar.

My dentist said, "Open up."
So, I told him my mother hated me, my father was a closeted gay, and my sister belongs to QAnon.

Joe Tickle wanted to marry the girl of his dreams.
She refused to take his surname.
Poor Tess.

Scientists say that, in the near future, brain transfers will be common.
Might get one. Then again, I might change my mind.

People are upset with the monk who saw the face of Jesus in a tub of margarine. They said, "I can't believe it's not Buddha!"

A cowboy was telling his grandson the secret to a long life:
"What I do is sprinkle a little gunpowder on my cereal every morning.
I'm 85!"
When he died a few years later, he left six children, fourteen grandchildren, and nine great-grandchildren.
And a 16-foot hole in the wall of the crematorium.

I spent ages trying to spell 'inconsequential' before I realized that it's not that important.

Indiana just announced a state-run anonymous sperm bank.
Although I question calling it "Hoosier Daddy?"

A T-Rex opened a handgun store here in town.
Deals solely in small arms.

Called the wife and asked her if she wanted me to pick up Bagels and
Lox on my way home from work. She just grunted.
Must still be pissed she let me name the twins.

Getting sick and tired of hearing Olympic athletes say how much work
they've put in and the sacrifices they've made.
What do they want, a medal?

Last night I dreamt I wrote *Lord of the Rings*.
My wife told me I was Tolkien in my sleep.

I don't remember many of the Motown groups.
I know maybe three... Four tops.

Sad about the great Italian chef who died. Pastaway.

What does Alexander the Great and Winnie the Pooh have in
common? Same middle name.

Had a job doing cell phone sales but got fired.
Guess it wasn't my calling.

Ollie and Ingrid were driving to their honeymoon in Minneapolis. Ollie gently put his hand Ingrid's leg. Ingrid leaned over and said, "Now that we're married, you can go further"
So, he drove to Duluth.

You can criticize Captain Hook all you want, but you gotta remember, he ran that ship single-handed!

I took my new puppy for his first shots today. He threw up everywhere. Maybe Tequila wasn't the best choice to start with?

My boss said, "You've been late three times this week. You know what that means?"
Apparently, "It's Wednesday?" wasn't the right answer.

Just found out Yoda's last name. It's Layheehoo.

"My wife and I are taking a Caribbean vacation."
"Jamaica?"
"No, she wants to go."

George Lucas and Jerry Seinfeld are teaming up on a movie!
Working title: 'Yoda, Yoda, Yoda'

The Feds were going to build a maximum-security prison in Alaska, but first they had to consider all of the frozen cons.

I bought a map of New England, and I'm planning on putting a pin in every place I visit this year. But first I need to visit the places in the upper left and right of the map so I can keep it on the wall.

Was dating a girl named Barb Dwyer, but we never got close.

If Lama with one L is a holy man, and llama with two L's is a beast of burden, what a three-L lama?
A wicked huge fire in Boston.

Just bought stock in a company that makes tennis balls.
High rate of return.

My neighbor built an altar, and each night he and his family worship plastic bags.
Sacreligious.

When Geronimo installed a light in his outhouse, he became the first man to wire a head for a reservation.

A driver of a semi carrying a shipment of wigs and toupees lost control on I-95, tipped the rig over on its side, and dumped the entire load of hair pieces. Police are rigorously combing the highway for evidence.

Big dog show the other day: A Yorkie took Best in Show, a Jack Russell took second, and a Scotty took third.
I think the judges had an all-terrier motive.

Music is just like candy.
It's great once you get rid of the rapper.

Tried to sneak into a *Star Trek* convention dressed as a doctor.
The security guy caught me and realized I wasn't the real McCoy.

Does Sasquatch get his sneakers from Big Foot Locker?

Russel Crowe and Sheryl Crow walk into a bar. The bartender calls
911 to report an attempted murder.

For the record, red wine and fish don't go well together.
Killed both my koi.

Haven't been to the gym in two years.
Went into the fitness protection program.

Hamlet developed a nasty cough, so he went to the doctor. Doc did a
full examination but just kept looking at the results. Hamlet couldn't
stand it anymore. "C'mon, Doc, TB or not TB?"

Been charging the family dog rent. He's a boarder collie.

My friend Obi and I played a game of *Star Wars* trivia.
Of course, Obi won.

I've become a fruitarian and only eat things that fall from trees.
For lunch today, I had an apple and a Robin.

Dear Lord,
Thank you for these noodles I'm about to eat.
Ramen.

When Quasimodo retired, he got a lump sum and six months back
pay.

Then there was the Mexican guy who had to take Xanax for Hispanic
attacks.

My gym instructor suggested I do lunges to keep fit.
It's a big step forward.

A genie granted me one wish, so I said, "I just want to be happy."
Now I'm living in a cottage with six dwarves and working in a mine.

Missing someone is a terrible feeling. Just ask any sniper.

The cashier at my local grocery store has a huge crush on me.
She checks me out every time I'm there.

Guy born with lobster-like hands got a job at Pizza Hut. They got him
on the crust station.

I hate people who can't let go of the past. Like debt collectors.

Didn't know that Pinocchio liked birds.
Someone said he has a woodpecker.

In high school, I went out for track but discovered I was deathly afraid
of the hurdles. Never got over it.

Two slices of bread got married. It was going well until they toasted
the bride and the groom.

Embarrassing. I farted in the Apple Store. They don't have Windows.

Running for office on a platform of banning pre-shredded cheese:
Make America Grate Again.

Clerk at Staples held off a robber with a labeling gun. Man.
Police are looking for a guy with a price on his head.

You're still gonna need a license to drive an electric car... it'll just need
to be current.

Dogs don't see it as being disobedient during their walk.
They see it as renegotiating the terms of their leash.

My wife started showing the first signs of Alzheimer's. She told me she doesn't remember what she ever saw in me.

The staff at my local supermarket are the worst. I used the self-service checkout and was named Employee of the Month twice.

I started using a new aftershave for men that enjoy their solitude. It's called 'Leave Me the Fah' cologne.

A woman knocked on my door and asked for a donation towards the public swimming pool. I gave her a glass of water. Support your community.

My daughter got a D in Science. When I inquired why, she said the teacher asked who Galileo was and "He's just a poor boy, from a poor family" was not the answer she was looking for.

The Institute of Unfinished Research has concluded that six out of ten people

I'm failing my marine biology class. My grade is below C level.

Tarzan's wife mailed me something to forward to ten friends for good luck. Jane letter.

First time in history all the buffaloes in Yellowstone gathered in one place, maybe 3,000. Rangers think it might be their Bisontennial.

The farmer who was on trial for stealing tons of seed has been found not guilty. His lawyers claimed the evidence was planted.

Reading a book on the history of lubricants. Non friction.

Beautiful day for golf. I broke 70 for the first time!
Yes, that is a lot of clubs.

So frustrating. I've asked twenty people what "idk" stands for, but no one seems to know.

A nurse walks into a bank after a 12-hour shift exhausted. She goes to write a check but pulls a rectal thermometer out of her pocket. She looks at the cashier and says, "Great, some asshole has my pen!"

Beastie Boys are releasing a five-CD set. Parts A-D are free, but you gotta fight for the right to part E.

Went to the most apathetic dance party last night. Everyone was raising their hands in the air... like they just didn't care.

Hamilton, holding a pistol and about to pace off: "Why are we doing this?"
Burr, holding a pistol and about to pace off: "Because you have dishonored me, and I hate your constant puns."
Hamilton: "Oh, a duel purpose."

Bigfoot's favorite exercise?
Sasquats.

Navigational equipment was stolen from the submarine base last night. Pretty sure the thief will be caught sonar or later.

My grandfather used to carve models of the Titanic. I can't find them anywhere, and, of course, he has no wreck collection.

Bought the latest SUV, and there's a button called 'Rear Wiper.'
Honestly, I'm afraid to push it.

For my birthday, my kids gave me a case of tongue depressors.
Gag gift.

Wonder if clouds ever look down on us and say, "Hey, look, that one's shaped like an idiot!"

Because of gas prices, potential buyers of the Honda Pilot have asked for a smaller model. So, Honda is introducing the Pilot Light.

What do hospital gowns and insurance have in common?
You think you're covered, but you're not.

Five ants moved into an apartment with five other ants. Now they are
tenants together.

I used to live a stone's throw away from a family who all died from
mysterious head injuries.

Applied for a job as a hit man today. Hours suck but killer benefits.

Create new password: Tomato
Confirm new password: Tomato
Passwords don't match.

When you're diagnosed with incontinence, you know urine trouble.

Two spies in a bar:
Him: "Can I buy you a drink?"
Her: "I'd tell you, but then I'd have tequila."

The Flat Earth Society is growing every day, with millions of members
around the globe.

How do snails fight?
They slug it out.

Hope Elon Musk never gets into a scandal because ElonGate would be really drawn out.

A horse walks into a bar and orders a whiskey. The bartender says, "You're in here every night. Do you think you might be an alcoholic?" The horse, "I don't think I am," and disappears.
The joke is based on Descartes' theory of "I think, therefore I am," but putting the explanation before the joke would be putting Descartes before the horse.

I spotted a couple of ducks in the park today.
The ranger made me leave and take my markers with me.

Gave a blind friend a cheese grater.
He said it's the most violent story he's ever read.

Had a doctor's appointment yesterday. Told him, every time I walk the dog my feet hurt so bad. He said I have to quit playing with my yo-yo.

I have a ridiculous sex drive. My girlfriend lived eighty miles away.

Read about a guy who was being booked by the police and had a heart attack. Cardiac arrest.

Wife: "I can't believe it. I haven't worn this in ten years and it still fits."
Me: "Yeah, well… it's a scarf."

Had a repairman come look at my printer after I heard music coming from it. He told me the paper was jamming.

Daffy Duck and Elmer Fudd break into a distillery.
Daffy turns to Elmer and says, "Is this whisky?"
Elmer says, "Yeth, but not as whisky as wobbing a bank!"

I asked my electrician to try and figure out why my lights kept going off. He refused.

Driving down the road and saw my ex. Funny how "I'd hit that" changed meaning over the years.

So many people are too judgmental. I can tell just by looking at them.

Used to play triangle in the local orchestra, but I quit.
Got to be one ting after another.

Guy who invented the throat lozenge passed away.
No coffin at his funeral.

A couple who own a Pot Emporium in Colorado are divorcing and fighting over the business. Judge will probably give them joint custody.

I applied for a job as a human cannonball and was fired the same day.

One proton won't speak to the other proton. He's mad atom.

I'm at the airport, and a man just collapsed on the luggage carousel. Wait, I think he's okay… He's coming around.

Romantic wife: "If you're sleeping, send me your dreams. If you're eating, send me a bite. If you're drinking wine, send me a sip. If you're laughing, send me your smile. If you're crying, send me your tears. I love you!"
Unromantic husband: "On the toilet. Please advise."

I was at the library when people began throwing Stephen King novels around. I could not figure out why. Then *It* hit me.

My doctor told me I was color blind.
Came completely out of the green.

I knew I was done with edibles when I was on the toilet and got frustrated trying to put on a seatbelt.

When I was in college, everyone bought Pioneer turntables and receivers. It was a common stereotype.

I've gained a lot of weight. But then, I've had a lot on my plate lately.

It's in the constitution that women should be free to wear sleeveless tops and dresses—the right to bare arms.

Saw a chameleon today. Obviously not a very good one.

Called my doctor and told him that I thought I have Monkey Pox.
He told me to swing by.

Mick walks into Paddy's barn and finds him dancing naked.
Mick says, "Paddy, what in blazes are ya doing?"
Paddy says, "Me and the missus haven't been getting on in the
bedroom."
Mick says, "So, why this?"
Paddy says, "Doc told me I needed to do something sexy to a tractor.

I should never have decided to become an archaeologist.
My life is in ruins.

Hopefully, the next big trend in music will be talent.

In Athens, no one wakes up until noon. Dawn is tough on Greece.

I asked my boss if I could leave half an hour early.
He said, "Only if you make up the time."
I said, "Okay. It's 35 past 50."

A roofer came into the ER complaining of extreme pain. The doctor came in with the guy's chart and said, "No need for an exam." The roofer responded, "How do you know what is wrong when you haven't examined me?" The doctor answered, "No brainer. You're a roofer; you've got Shingles."

I dropped a 4-pack of margarine on my foot three months ago and it still hurts. I can't believe it's not better.

Reading about the woman who tried to cut off her husband's penis but cut his leg. She was only charged with a misdawiener.

Do Siamese twins who love baseball only go to double-headers?

Shortage reported on Kielbasa and Brats.
People are preparing for the wurst.

Got thrown out of the IKEA store.
I asked the clerk, "Is this desk finished?"
She replied, "No, it's Swedish."
That's when the fight started.

The Powerball jackpot tonight is one tank of gas, a quart of baby formula, two rolls of toilet paper and a single sheet of half-inch plywood.

Set up a booth at the mall where I tie people's shoelaces for them for a dollar. Next year, I'll file my taxes as a knot-for-profit.

My neighbor with the huge tits was out watering the garden topless again. Wonder if his wife knows?

After my prostrate exam, the doctor left, and the nurse came in. She whispered three words no man wants to hear: "Who was that?"

My girlfriend looks superhot without glasses.
So, I stopped wearing them.

The best advice my father gave me was, when you're over fifty, never trust a fart.

Wal-Mart announced they will be putting dental offices in their stores with an express lane for people with ten teeth or less.

What do bullfighters use to keep their skin soft? Oil of ¡Ole!

Ended up having to courier packages of food to my former girlfriend. She lost her job. Fed Ex.

Amazon fired me because of my nose problem.
Hey, they hired me as a picker...

With the NBA and NHL seasons over, one network is showing the World Origami Championships. Paperview.

My auto insurance company is the worst. They question everything. It's like I have a $500 debatable.

Bought a new car, a Rolls. Not a Rolls Royce, a Rolls. Can only go downhill.

On top of that, the warranty in the contract is six pages long, most of it called the 'Nudist Clause.' Nothing is covered.

Guy showing his buddy his new golf ball: "This golf ball is state of the art. You just can't lose this ball. If it goes in the rough, it beeps. It glows in the dark, it floats in water, and it has a built in GPS." Friend asks, "Where did you get it from?"
"Found it."

Travel is getting rough. One airline, in order to compete, is now claiming that their planes are the cleanest. Their ads show them putting deodorant under the wings.

I bought the latest iteration of the Magic 8-Ball. It's of the time. No matter what you ask it, the answer comes up, "No idea."

Do you think the chef at the Last Supper ever worked again?

Michelangelo took seven years to paint the ceiling of the Sistine Chapel, and no one said a word. Strong union.

Got a tattoo of Italy on my chest. Didn't hurt that much, but now I have sore Naples.

Read a fascinating book on the history of milk.
Well, actually, I just skimmed it.

When I was young, we were so poor, I only had bits of rope to eat for breakfast. We would skip lunch.

Sci-fi is wrong. Aliens won't visit our planet.
We have terrible ratings... only one star.

Found a spider in the house. Wife said take him out instead of killing him, so I did. Nice guy. Had a couple of drinks. He's a web designer.

Weird new trend in the office where people are naming food in the fridge. Ate a sandwich today named Linda.

Reading that NASA sent a probe to Uranus.
Why does everyone giggle when I tell them that?

My landlord said he needs to talk to me about how high my heating bill is. I told him, "My door is always open."

The navy is laying off non-essential personnel, including barbers.
A complete crew cut.

Used to be in a band. Long time ago. We called ourselves Hinges.
We opened for The Doors.

A woman awakes during the night to find that her husband is not in bed. She puts on her robe and goes downstairs to look for him. She finds him sitting at the kitchen table with a hot cup of coffee in front of him. He appears to be in deep thought, just staring at the wall. She watches as he wipes a tear from his eye and takes a sip of his coffee.
"What's the matter, dear," she whispers as she steps into the room.
"Why are you down here at this time of night?"
The husband looks up from his coffee, "It's the 20th Anniversary of the day we met."
She can't believe he has remembered and starts to tear up. The husband continues, "Do you remember twenty years ago when we started dating? I was eighteen, and you were only sixteen," he says solemnly.
Once again, the wife is touched to tears. "Yes, I do" she replies.
The husband pauses. The words were not coming easily. "Do you remember when your father caught us in the back seat of my car?"
"Yes, I remember," said the wife, lowering herself into the chair beside him.
The husband continued. "Do you remember when he shoved the shotgun in my face and said, 'Either you marry my daughter, or I will send you to prison for 20 years?'"
"I remember that, too," she replied softly.
He wiped another tear from his cheek and said, "I would have gotten out today."

"I bet you can't tell me something that will make me both happy and sad at the same time," a husband says to his wife.
She thinks about it for a moment and then responds, "Your penis is bigger than your brother's."

My penis was in the *Guinness Book of World Records*… until the librarian made me take it out.

The difference between chickpeas and garbanzo beans?
Trump wouldn't pay $500 for a hooker to garbanzo bean on his face.

People know about Anne Boleyn, but few know she had a brother, Tenpin.

My favorite childhood memory was building sandcastles with my grandpa… until my mom put the urn up too high to reach.

Got a cold the other day while riding on a carousel.
It's something going around.

I have the body of a porn star. All my clothes say XXX.

My son was going to major in the study of archaeology but soon changed. Said it felt dated.

"Doctor, I can't hear out of my left ear."
"Are you sure?"
"Yes, I'm definite."

My wife is complaining because I don't buy her flowers.
Jeez, I didn't even know she sold flowers.

Just switched from eating venison to eating pheasant. Game changer.

My therapist suggested I write a note to my wife about my addiction to
magic shows. I just can't pick up the Penn and Teller.

Said to the girl at the checkout, "Can I get this any cheaper? It's got
today's date on it."
She said, "Look, do you want the newspaper or not?"

German guy sees a dog drowning in the river and jumps in to save it.
A passerby yells, "Are you a vet?"
German says, "A vet? I'm fuckin' soaked!"

Heard that most accidents happen within two miles of your home…
So, I moved.

Went to my 50th high school reunion. Unfortunately, all my friends got
so old and fat, no one recognized me.

People say I'm lazy. I'm not lazy; I'm a relaxaholic.

"Who's that girl you were with?"
"Someone I know from working at the school."
"Teacher?"
"Didn't have to."

My exercise routine includes crunches twice a day.
Captain in the morning, and Nestle's in the evening.

Due to supply chain issues, vendors are saying that artificial
Christmas trees may be in short supply later this year.
Sounds like fake yews.

Watched some Jewish porn last night. Forty minutes of begging, three
minutes of sex, and seventeen minutes of guilt. Good flick.

A woman I know confused her birth control pills with her Valium.
She now has ten kids but couldn't care less.

Bought a dog and named him Egypt because he leaves a pyramid in
every room.

My acne is getting out of control. Yesterday, I was walking on the
street and a blind man tried to read my face.

Miss Piggy is the beneficiary of Kermit's life insurance policy. She just
has to wait until he croaks.

What's an Italian suppository? An innuendo.

You can make your waterbed bouncier by adding spring water.

Told my boss that three huge companies were after me, and I needed a large pay raise. He asked, "Which companies?"
I said, "Electric, Gas, and Water."

Dated this girl who said I push her buttons.
If that were true, you'd think I'd have found 'mute' by now.

I caught my wife sleeping with her personal trainer.
I told her this isn't working out.

A biology teacher grew human vocal cords from stem cells in the lab.
The results speak for themselves.

Ever since I was a kid, I've had the ability to guess what's inside a wrapped present.
I know. It's a gift.

Started reading a book about Fort Knox, but I'm finding it really hard to get into…

The doctor prescribed me anti-gloating cream.
Not sure if I should rub it in.

Monday starts Diarrhea Appreciation week. Runs until Friday.

Saw two canoes racing on the lake yesterday, when one just veered
and plowed into the other one.
Rowed rage.

We shot off fireworks last night, but man, the cost skyrocketed!

Make little things count. Teach math to midgets.

Hear about the Eskimo that sat on the ice too long? Polaroids.

She has the body of a 22-year-old. A 22-year-old Volvo.

If Mama Cass had shared her sandwich with Karen Carpenter, they'd
both be alive today.

My wife met me at the door wearing sexy underwear.
Unfortunately, she was coming home.

My sex life is terrible. I called a phone sex line, and the voice said,
"Not tonight, I have an earache."

Went to my eye doctor because I thought there was something wrong.
I kept seeing an insect spinning around my head.
He told me there's a bug going round.

Bought a container of powdered water. Just don't know what to add.

I said 'no' to drugs. They just wouldn't listen.

Went to a Chinese restaurant last night. Great ambiance, but the lights were far too bright. So, the manager decided to dim sum.

I have a pen that will write underwater.
It can write other words, too.

I was fired from my taxi job. People evidently don't appreciate it when you go the extra mile for them.

While doing a jigsaw puzzle, I accidentally swallowed one of the puzzle parts. Through meditation and ex-lax, I was able to find inner piece.

Teacher: "Class, can anyone make a sentence using the word 'fascinate'?"
Johnny: "My dad's shirt has ten buttons, but 'cause of his fat belly, he can only fasten eight."

Huh. Just realized that the actor who played Wilson in *Castaway* was the same actor that was in all those volleyball scenes in *Top Gun*!

I took a sexual harassment course last week.
Think I'm gonna be pretty good at it!

Three little old ladies took a bottle of bourbon to a baseball game.
By the bottom of the fifth, the bags were loaded.

Despite his reputation, I've always found Frankenstein's monster to be
a level-headed guy.

My wife woke up screaming, "Help! I'm giving birth to Sir Galahad's
horse!" She's been having these knightmares a lot lately.

My wife told me I was obsessed with Billy Joel.
I told her, "You may be right, I may be crazy..."
Then she said I needed to get rid of my Hall and Oates collection.
But I can't go for that.

Ate a piece of cured ham, and it was fine.
No idea what it was ever sick with.

Discovered that Hamburger Helper only works if the hamburger is
really ready to accept help.

Tried counting sheep to get to sleep last night... I got to 500 and lost
interest, so I went back home and got back into bed.

I always get my pizza delivered.
Who knows why they put liver on it in the first place.

Duct-taped a dictionary to each end of a broomstick and started lifting weights with it. I'm getting more defined every day.

A man thinks he is a dog, so he goes to see a psychiatrist. "It's terrible," says the man. "I walk around on all fours, I keep barking in the middle of the night, and I can't go past a lamppost without peeing." "Okay," says the psychiatrist. "Get on the couch." "I'm not allowed on the couch."

My neighbor pointed out several slugs in my garden and advised me to go and get some salt. Guy will eat anything.

When I was growing up, my mother used to bathe me in cheap Australian Lager. It wasn't until later that I discovered I'd been fostered.

Seeing 50 Cent and Nickelback in concert next week! Tickets are only 45¢!

My fear of needles kept me from getting into any IV league schools.

The invisible man marries the invisible woman. Their kids are nothing to look at.

Checked my home insurance policy. Apparently, if my duvet is stolen in the middle of the night, I'm not covered.

Nothing is built in America anymore. Just bought a new TV and it said, "Built in Antenna." I don't even know where that is...

Great example of oral contraceptive:
I asked a girl to go to bed with me, and she said no.

Next time I want to send an idiot on an errand, I'll just go myself.

Why do Jewish men get circumcised?
Because no Jewish woman would touch anything that's not 20% off.

John Wayne's *The Searchers*... so unrealistic. Not a single flashlight.

Saw a guy on the subway playing a didgeridoo. Nice version of 'Dancing Queen'. An Abbariginal.

Scottish men wear kilts because sheep can hear a zipper a mile away.

How does a union boss tell his son a story?
"Once upon a time and a half..."

When my back is sore, I go to an Egyptian doctor, my Cairopractor.

I swallowed some food coloring.
Doctor says I'll be fine, but I feel like I dyed a little inside.

Took an air balloon ride. Lovely. Played music, all kinds.
Jazz, classical. Just one kind not allowed: pop.

My Grandpa's wishes were to be cremated, so we did just that.
He urned it.

Son: "I watched a guy do fifty pull-ups. Can you do that, Dad?"
Father: "Of course. Not to brag, but I could probably watch a guy do
one hundred pull-ups."

If A is for Apple, and B is for Banana, what is C for?
Plastic explosives.

I accidentally handed my wife a glue stick instead of chap stick.
She still isn't talking to me.

The day passed quickly as we lingered over our Mexican custard. It's
true... time really flies when you're having flan.

What pronouns does chocolate use? Her/she

Got in trouble and have to do community service picking up trash. I
asked about training. Guy said I'd pick it up.

I love that show about finding your roots, but I could never afford a
DNA test. So, I announced that I hit the lottery, and soon every relative
I had showed up.

I am of German ancestry. Half of my relatives can be traced back to Hamburg, the others Frankfurt. When we get together, it's a real picnic!

It's hot, but at least it's not snowing.
Imagine shoveling snow in this heat.

Watch *Jaws* backwards, and it's a heartwarming story of a shark who gives arms and legs to disabled people.

Got kicked out of a karaoke bar last night for trying to sing 'Danger Zone' five times. Exceeded the maximum Loggins attempts.

It is fairly easy to prevent ladies from drinking laundry soap, but it is much more difficult to detergent.

Went to the Grand Canyon and rode a donkey down into it. Then someone threw a rock at me, and I fell. Stoned off my ass.

Just as an FYI: It's no longer called 'box wine.'
The term is now 'cardboardeaux.'

That Indian restaurant is so secretive. If you work there, you have to sign a legal agreement not to share their flatbread recipe. Standard naan disclosure agreement.

Are slugs divorced snails?

I melted an ice cube just by staring at it.
Although, it took longer than I thought it would.

Aladdin was banned from racing his carpet.
Performance enhancing rugs.

My wife crashed the car again. She said the other guy was on his
mobile phone and drinking a beer. The cops told her he can do that
while he's in his own living room.

Freddie Mercury, Venus Williams, and Bruno Mars walk into a bar.
They didn't planet that way.

Shakespeare used to chew the ends of his pencils so much that you
couldn't tell if it was 2B or not 2B.

I just finished reading a suspense novel about a Rubik's cube.
It was full of twists and turns.

Made in United States
North Haven, CT
22 March 2024

50240830R20064